Thank you to my husband Ross, for his love and support in helping me to collect the necessary photographs, in a one-day marathon at Chelsea; thank you also to Brooke, our graphic designer, who works her magic in making the books ready for printing, and to Paul, our web technician who also works his magic in keeping the websites active and responsive.

It's 2023 and there we were, waiting at the station to catch the train into Paddington, London, and then, we travelled on the underground train to Sloane Street, Station…

The excitement was mounting as many people started to leave the train for the walk to the Chelsea Flower Show.

There he was, a man in a brightly coloured shirt offering lifts in his rikshaw, the opportunity to ride through London in this way was too great to pass up and the ride was excellent, seeing sights often taken for granted when in the car…!

At the gate, where many people patiently waited, the day had begun and what a day we had in the beautiful spring sun…

Please see the following pages to follow our journey and the beauty of a magnificent flower show –

The Magic of Chelsea

The Respect They Deserve...

Isn't about time we gave the respect back to our native insects, their environments, and homes?

For well over two hundred years our insects have been in their personal fight to survive. They don't have a voice, they cannot shout, scream, and make a noise when their homes are destroyed, the only sign they give, is when they no longer exist...!

The emphasis for the 2023 Chelsea Flower Show was on native fields and meadow flowers and grasses, and how refreshing to see the abundance of differently coloured flowers, their shape, form, texture, and vibrancy; some petals glistened as the rays of sunshine caught their movement in the soft spring breeze, and what a treat for any human being to enjoy the moments of this year's Chelsea Flower Show...!

They Want to Survive...

The butterfly you see, has many jobs to do, not only the will to survive but to pollenate the flowers it visits but to make babies for next year too…!

Its time spent is only a few, with so many jobs, and soon, this beautiful creature will need to support the new…

So fragile its wings and glorious too, but delicate as fairy dust, and now too often, too few…!

The butterfly has many messages to give, for it is the story, the story to live…!

Like mothers, from nature we find, the will to produce their babies each year, and to do just that, they need to know the earth will be kind…!

For once the babies are new, the mum's job is done, its short life is lived, for its legacy it leaves, its babies for next year, the flowers it pollinates and the beauty it gives…!

When you see your next butterfly, please take the time to ponder, and then wonder, not only at the joy of the sight, but at the work it does with all its might….!

If you have purchased this book without its cover, it may be a stolen book.

Neither the publisher or the author is under any obligation to provide professional services in anyway, legal, health or in any form which is related to this book, its contents advice or otherwise.

The law and practices vary from country to country and state to state.

If legal or professional information is required, the purchaser, or the reader should seek the information privately and best suited to their particular needs, and circumstances.

The author and publisher specifically disclaim any liability that may be incurred from the information within this book.

All rights reserved. No part of this book, including the interior design, images, cover design, diagrams, or any intellectual property (IP), icons and photographs may be reproduced or transmitted in any form by any means (electronic, photocopying, recording or otherwise) without the prior permission of the publisher. ©

Copyright© 2023 MSI Australia

All rights reserved.

ISBN: 978-0-6457284-7-7

Published by How2Books
Under licence from MSI Ltd, Australia
Company Registration No: 96963518255
NSW, Australia

See our website: www.how2books.com.au
Or contact by email: sales@how2books.com.au
Covers and Copyright owned by MSI, Australia

MSI acknowledges the author and images, text and photographs used in this book.

10% of the sale of each book helps to support Diabetes Type One and Cancer Research.

THE BACK STORY

Six O'clock on the dot, the taxi arrives! The early autumn morning in Australia is beautiful in April with a slight change in the colour of the leaves on the trees, as they turn from green to slight gold. From the drop off at the station in Bowral, New South Wales, and as we sit on the train on the way to Sydney Airport, it's time to inhale, take a deep breath, and the time to think about the journey we've just begun...

With so many kilometres to travel, there is no time to stop, the hustle and bustle of the time, keeps us alert and ready to go at a 'drop of a hat!' Trains, airports, rental cars, all with many people making their way to different worldwide destinations!

Most faces are concerning with the look, 'I hope this is the right way to go, or is this the flight we take...?' And so it is, the long-haul from one side of the planet to the other...! Regardless of lengthy waits, airport crowds and long-distance travel, how many generations have had the privilege of flying across the oceans, baron areas of land below, and still be served food on the flight and a glass or two of wine or a coffee when needed...?

The technology needed to bring our books to our readers is mesmerizing and yet, we use it without much thought. Once my brain accepts, we are living in the here and now, the flight journey has come to an end, and we are there in the Baggage Hall at Heathrow Airport...

It's amazing how the scramble, each person goes through, to collect their bags and it never seems to change! We have waited for bags, that don't appear because they have been left at an airport in Australia...! We have also been fortunate enough to have the bags come around on the first baggage carousel to circulate...! The bags collected; we make our way to the hire car. and what a relief to finally sit in the passenger seat and, at last, to see the different greens on the forming leaf buds as they show their many different greens. Just one sunny day was needed to bring the trees of the South of England into magnificent colour. Alas, it was too cold to allow that to happen...!

It was the 14th of April, we were there, at the 15th Century Notley Abbey, and to see our beautiful Goddaughter married. The weather was cold and wet, but the bride was radiant and gorgeous. Many weeks pass and we are on the train heading to The Chelsea Flower Show. Memories rush into my head, how the time has flown since I did my training in London to become a florist, and yet my heart and mind long for the colours, textures, and vibrancy of the flowers I will later see that day!

I'm jolted into the current moment, we are there, at Sloane Street, Station, and the crowds start to stand up from their train seats and want to step out onto the platform. Though there are many people, order is a priority for the excited crowd. No grim faces could be seen, just people happy to enjoy the moments of the day!

Emerging into the bright sunlight from the darkness of the station, my eyes were transfixed on a man wearing a brightly coloured floral shirt; he was the rikshaw driver and I was determined to make the most of the day, I persuaded my husband to part with, what was meant to be a fifteen-pound ride into a twenty-pound ride…, at the end of the trip…!

It was wonderful to see these parts of London, not normally seen when we are looking for parking or on a busy London bus!

As we travelled on our short journey to the flower show, I couldn't help thinking about my own studies, not only as a florist in London, but one amazing year spent at the Canberra School of Art where I studied 20th century art history and sculpting. These studies have brought together the knowledge I now have in the ability to make meaningful comments about the exhibits on display in 2023.

Now, to our readers, please enjoy this lovely new edition of 'The Magic of Chelsea'.

Christine

Christine Thompson-Wells, Author of Many Books
CEO, How2Books &
Full Potential Education & Training
BA Education, Dip of Teaching, MACEA,
CPD Accredited Education

Content   Page

The Reason Why…?	1
The Reason Why – Poem	2
People On the Move	3
The Clematis as it Grows	4
Clematis – Poem	5
Sculpture	6
Sculpture – Mesmerizing Creations	7
Gentle Thoughts of Childhood	9
A Time to Think and Take a Moment – Poem	11
The Inspiration of Shape	12
From Flowing Form to the Movement of Glass – A Combination of Glass and Steel	15
With Impression – The Merging of Water and Sculpture	17
Paul Richardson	19
From the Rock it Comes – Poem	20
From Rock	21
James Parker – Sculpture	23
Light in the Garden	25
A Day of Fun	27
The Art of Floristry Design	28
The Art of Floristry Design…	29
Floristry and Floral Art	43
The Floris – Poem	44
The Mush Room	47
The Mush Room…	48
Shapes, Colour & Texture	50
Garden Display	51
Show Gardens	52
Titled, 'A Letter from a Million Years Past…'	53
Coolness of Colour – The Myeloma Garden	55
The Natural Affinity Garden	57
Turning Rubbish to Treasure	59
Gracious and Cool	61
Daisies, Daisies, Daisies…	62
More Choices of Cost-Effective Garden Designs	63
The Magic of Space – Poem	66
The Great Pavilion	67
Expectations	68
Upside-Down Flowers…! The Yellow Brick Road	69
Soft and Demure	71
Cor-Ten – Popular and Different	72
Alliums Galore	75
Amaryllis Lilies	77
Rosies, Rosies, Rosies	79
Big Show – 'GOLD' Disbud Chrysanthemums	81

	Page
Daffodils & Narcissus – a Sign of Spring	83
Clematis – Pictures of Perfection	85
Picture of Perfection	87
The Night – Poem	88
Succulents and Cacti	89
The Magic of the Moment	91
Semi-Tropical Flowers	94
Trinidad and Tobago	97
Zantedeschia – Colours to Make Your Heart Sing	98
Incredible Orchids	100
Oh, and Then There Were Tulips…!	102
Gladiolus	104
Sunshine and Lilies – Who Could Ask for More…?	106
Dahlia Beach	109
Iris or Flag Iris…?	110
The Iris – Poem	113
The Pleasure of Delphiniums	114
Amazing Maple	116
The Water Garden	117
The Salad Bowl	118
Old Fashioned Violas are Back and in Abundance	119
Shots of Magic	121
Pretty Gardens	122
Different Gardens – Different Approaches to Gardening	126
Different Combinations & Peace of Mind	127
Sweet Peas	128
Who Remembers Wallflowers?	129
Gardens to Capture Dreams	130
Splendid Grasses	131
Bonsai and Perfection	133
Another Reign Begins	136
Garden Accessories	137
The Ancient Art of Pebble Laying	138
Interesting Stalls – The Delphinium Society	139
Susan Entwistle Art	140
Bee The Change	141
Mr Fothergill's	142
Containers Made from Husks	143
The Peony Girl	144
Clothes of the Future	145
Treats of the Show	147
The Reason Why…? The Magic of Chelsea	152
Other Books that May Interest You	153

The Reason Why...?

Since 1804, the RHS Chelsea Flower Show, has been an annual event. Originally it was called The Great Spring Show.

In 1913, it was moved to its present location at the Royal Hospital, Chelsea.

It's the glamour and excitement that makes the flower show such an exciting event. It is the event in many people's calendars each year that allows the show to be the success it is in the twenty-first century.

The Royal Hospital, Chelsea, is home to about three hundred British Army veterans, which include both men and women, all of which call the hospital, 'Home'.

Many of the veterans have served in Cyprus, Northern Ireland, the Falklands War, and the Second World War, from (1939-1945).

Originally, and the precursor to the establishment of the hospital in 1677, it was established for officers of disbanded regiments, soldiers with injuries, which was the original force by Sir Stephen Fox (1627-1716). Royal patronage was added to the establishment by King Charles II in 1682. The purpose of the hospital was to establish a retreat for war veterans.

The Reason Why…?

So many times, we see, the people that have served…
To keep our lands free…!

Through years of battle, we are here, not by chance you know, but by
dedication of the people we cannot see…!

The numbers too great to count, but sometimes we may reflect, on those past
lives that allow us to live our daily lives…
Though they may be humble, we are at least free…!

With the tradition we hold, those lives once lived, and may we not forget
the enormous price they paid…!

To allow us to make the choices we freely make as from day to day
We learn….

The wonders of the moments, some of the past veterans did not
have time to yearn…!

For this is the reason, that so many can enjoy, the wonders of the
Chelsea Show that so many have not had the time
to know…!

Many people want to see the wonders of the show, and
yet, it's time to stop, reflect, and the Reason Why
we know….!

In Remembrance.

People on the Move
The Enjoyment of the day...

With so much to see and such a short window of time to see the stands and exhibits, each moment was a special moment spent at the show. And from the crowd numbers, many other visitors may have felt also, that way...!

The Clematis as it Grows

The clematis is such an extraordinary flower; it has a delicate and petal combination that holds your vision as you look deeply into the flower's centre.

In this beautiful photograph, the gentle pink hue, with a slight hint of deep maroon towards the ovary of the flower shows this beauty.

Gentle petals shown, show soft the white outer petals leading the eye through the deeper pink and veins of the petal, which all lead to the magnificent centre of filaments and anthers, such a beautiful combination of colour it also makes one think of the porcelain china once used for afternoon teas and of years gone by...!

This new cultivar named the Duchess of Wessex displayed a magnificent show of such fine flowers.

This variety had a soft, but delicious scent and created a soothing combination within such a busy location.

Clematis come in many colours from purples to soft pinks and stunning whites. Most develop a woody type of stem as they mature.

Clematis

She holds her head in wonder as she flirts within the show…!

With many colours she flaunts, and just to let us know…!
Many single flowers to display, and hold our vision so, and as we gasp and say 'show some more…'
Our hearts will gently soar…!

The mischief she holds so dear, is part of her lasting charm…
For within such beauty, there cannot be any harm….!

As new petals unfurl and old flowers wither in the sun…
The short and beauty of the day is speckled with great fun…!

For porcelain the petals seem on appearance as you look, but beyond the delicate structure is the story within the book…!

Like so many flowers before her grew…
and so beautiful, and alas, only now, it is too few…!

The clematis, as we see it in the show, and what a sight…
for those simple petals will fade throughout the night…!

And it is with memories we linger of a spectacle once seen…
The clematis is recharging for the show she was so keen…!

And for next year she flowers again and the beauty to behold
for the beauty within this flower is magnificent and bold…!

Sculpture

With many creative displays in this year's show, it is difficult to identify a favourite! We apologise, if we have missed your designs, but we can only offer so much space within our book.

The ideas within the sculptures that follow, were major talking points, and points of inspiration, not only for the show visitors, but we are sure, for the creators of the masterpieces.

Sculpture – Mezmerising Creations

The show did not miss out on presenting many amazing sculptures this year, with many representations, show the beauty of the planet and the birds that fly the skies.

Opposite, mezmerising shapes, all giving their own version of our planet and the flight of the swallows.

Swallows travel many thousands of miles and arrive in the United Kingdom, from Africa, in April each year. They are ready to make their return journey by about September.

A delightful sculpture gives us the story of the swallows' flight...!

Considering we had a luggage weight we needed to think about, it would be nice to just slip one of these magnificent sculptures into the handbag, but alas, too big for such a thought or consideration...!

Opposite, the aqua colour of cut leaf shapes allows you to wonder and yet the softness of the colour, is, restful for the eye...!

To keep the orb or globe shape so perfectly balanced, round, and yet, to give the appearance of almost a lace of iron or steel work, within the sculpture, allows us to think about the gentleness of the force within the materials used in this display.

In the below sculpture, the added use of water creates a gentle flow of movement, and softness of sound….!

Gentle Thoughts of Childhood

How many times can we reflect on those special moments when we were children?

The peace and solitude of the moment may have been after playing or just taking time to think on a sleepy summer afternoon...!

In these photographs, perhaps, the children have just had a paddle in a cool mountain stream, or maybe, it was just time to take their shoes off after school...!

Whatever the occasion, the sculptures of Brian Alabaster, makes me stop to think of my own English childhood and those very special days of warm sunshine, cool grass to sit on and the gentle blowing of a summer breeze...!

Goodness, what treasured memories these children's images brings to the surface of my mind...!

Hot summer days and the freedom of the countryside all come into the mind as we stop and look at wonderful, and lifelike sculptures.

The sculptures show the movement of the children and the freedom they are feeling from sitting quietly reading a book, feeling the pleasure of cool fresh water running on the young and growing body, or from running in the fields; all such movement is seen in the figures we see in these photographs.

The images bring back such bold and vivid memories of an English summer.

In the sculpture opposite, I can remember my own experiences, and too, recall, my own hair in a ponytail bouncing, as I ran to catch either the bus or running through a field on the way home from school...!

Last year we featured Brian's beautiful sculpture of three children climbing the book staircase entitled: 'The Next Step', this sculpture is now installed in Alperton, Brent. That sculpture was one of the impressions of great physical movement by the children as the climbed each separate pile of books.

A Time to Think and Take a Moment...

Time does not stand still, for the moments of those summer days,
are distant to recall...!

It takes the magic of the moment, and a chance of reflection to
know the journey from that time...!

We may have many mountains set in front of us, and some of us do fall...!

But it is about the moment and the way that we recall...
for many mountains are a hurdle but meant to overcome...!

For that is part of life and sent to make us strong, and yet,
it is easy to find another route...

That was not the intention, and a lesson will not be learnt,
some people feel the anger and some, their heart is burnt...!

It is the lesson of the journey, that makes it all worthwhile, and knowing
if you see it through, many wrongs can be the start of something new...!

For it is in the moment that we hear the magic of the song...!

Do not give up the moment, when life is such a hurdle to restore, but
know that with every moment, there is magic in achievement and helps
you build your core...

Life has many bounties, and some may not know...
but it is the moment and the time to think it through...!

That allows us to be creative in all the thoughts and actions that we take
and do...!

For the magic of the moment, if not understood, may become too few...!

Live, Laugh and Love the Moments.

The Inspiration of Shape

Since the human mind started to collect information and put ideas together, we have been transfixed about shape. Whether it is the shape of the female form, the leaves on a tree, birds in the sky, shape is all around us – shape is shape and has form, is three-dimensional and above all else, incredibly interesting to observe.

These sculptures by John O'Connor, give the human eye a different perspective on the human anatomy.

Opposite, is it any wonder we often hear people say, *'I could do that standing on my head...!'*

Regardless of the expression, it is highly unlikely that many people could create such a piece of beautiful art, especially on their head!

In this piece, 'Earth Elevation', the sheer expression within the art form gives us the impression, 'If we think about an idea long enough, we can reach great feats within the human mind and the accomplishments we can achieve.

Opposite, 'Mixed Media' is the title of this sculpture. John uses a combination recycled plastic bottles and highly versatile resin. By adding large quantities of ground dusts to the resins, it offers a variety of finishes.

Some sculptures are produced from iron, bronze, marble, copper, and have slate finishes.

There is a great drive of energy in all John's work. Some of which gives the viewer a feeling of taking off.

Other sculpted pieces lead the eye to the stars, the feelings of magnitude and the wonders we have within our planet of earth. Each of the sculptures lead the mind to thinking deeply about how fortunately we are to be living and experiencing great forms of art.

With such exceptional craftmanship and the insight to create the human form, which takes our vision of the work to extensions of thinking within each viewing, it is difficult to comprehend how a single person can visualise the work and then create it, thus, allowing us all to appreciate the beauty it offers.

From Flowing Form to the Movement of Glass – A Combination of Glass and Steel

Two such amazing materials working together: stainless steel and glass…!

From time immemorial, the human brain has been intrigued by shape and the extension of how objects are seen and then transcended into images seen on cave walls, or later. Then human capability progressed to cut glass which allowed them to make stained glass windows and further expressions within human emotion.

Every piece of art created, is an extension of the artist's emotion and their perspective of their life experiences…!

Molten glass, when produced, takes a creative mind and many years of working with the medium to understand how glass flows. It is not only the flow but the clever use of colour in swirls that make the opposite sculpture so interesting to observe.

It is as if we are taken back to the running of water, the flow of sea currents, and the mesmerising actions of sea surf, all of which are encased in pure stainless steel. The steel is sharp, definite in shape and almost clinical which adds to the entrancement hidden in the combination of materials used and cleverness in the use of shape.

In the below glass circles, unlike the previously spoken about glass sculpture, that had movement in the swirls and shapes seen, however, this artwork has lines of straight glass seen, all of which are encased in the roundness of a circle. It is almost a combination of contradictions which make the design so interesting.

Making a further study of the two circles, one is drawn to the autumn colours of a further round shape, and then to the blues and slight autumn tones of the lower circle.

Introducing blues allows the circle to appear soothing to the eye and yet, the strength of the glass lines draws us to look at the autumn browns which lead the eye to the top circle. It is a clever use of colour when one takes the time to linger and enjoy the energy, work and talent involved in creating such a combination of colour and line.

While at the Canberra School of Art, and during my floristry training, I learnt, '...*a curve is a deviation of a line,*' and in the above the circle emphasises that very description.

Opposite, running water and round shapes of glass are a clever combination used in this sculpture.

The sound of flowing water can contribute to the wellbeing of our senses: relaxation, peacefulness, and quality brain time...

With Impression – The Merging of Water and Sculpture

As seen in the last photograph of glass, when used as a key feature with water, the combination makes for solace and peace of the human mind.

In the opposite photograph, it is the combination of the water lily shape and the use of water that enhances the richness of the design.

Ian Gill, is both a blacksmith and artist. His work is creative and yet, he can take minimal material to create a combination of movement and expression.

By using creative expression, Ian enhances his ideas into his work which allows the movement of magic to take place. The anodised metal water lily in the above photograph, gives a mystical energy and takes the eye to the peripheral of the design. Adding the water to grey, almost cloudy atmosphere of the visual expectations here, we have a chance to look at the curving petals as the flower unfurls, thus, allowing the water to flow.

With so many water features in one display, it was difficult to stop looking at the creativity of the moment.

Water, obviously playing a big part in the inspiration and creativity to design and make the sculptures would take many hours of work. Like most art creation, the concept and art form must first be the inspiration of the artist for the design, thus, this would allow creative energy to flow...!

With so much artistic expression from the visual abundance of bull rushes to the image of a nursing mother.

The bull rushes show a combination of water and the significance the water plays of allowing bullrushes to thrive in many natural waterways.

The viewer is led to the movement and humanity of the image below of a mother and child.

The child is an infant; the tilt of the mother's head shows concern and love for the baby she holds.

The image is created by using just five pieces of metal, and yet the emotion it evokes in a viewer of the scene is both capturing and memorable.

The fact that the mother appears to be sitting on a swing, in a possible garden setting, also adds to the ambiance of the overall impression one is left with.

From the complexity of natural shapes being taken from nature to the development of the human shape nursing a child can only be seen as a true expression of human emotion.

Paul Richardson

With so much sculpture on offering, it was a bombardment and enjoyment of the visual senses...

Opposite, the zinc coated metal disk shows off an incredible volume of work undertaken to create this almost effervescent image of steel.

With the puffiness of the steel shaped circles, it gives one the impression of a dandelion in seed, which is about to send the seeds into the wind to recreate dandelions for the next season.

Whilst different light at different times of the day plays an integral part of this delicate design, it should not be forgotten, the sculpture is made from steel.

Photograph courtesy, Paul Richardson, Garden Steel Sculptures

From the Rock it Comes...

The metal it comes from is far from thought...
As we look at the wonder brought...!

When the rock was formed, many millions of years ago...
It was possibly not the intention that art would be created, and there, the human mind would extend and grow...!

And so it is, the creations we have, not only in the artistic light...
but also in the form of war and fight...!

When such beauty can be seen, it is the wonder of the rock,
from which it comes, can be used for inspiration to acknowledge
both the splendour and the flight...!

Through past centuries, the rock has been there, without little wonder,
without little care...!

And yet, the human mind extends, with so much emphasis on creative thought, but alas, we can use the rock for both expression and love, and yet, it can be used for none of the above...!

To create from rock, the shapes of unfurling leaves to be seen, and yet, when we stop and think,

That rock now used, can be part of the chain,
and contributes to human pain...!

For without the rock, wars would not exist, weapons would not be made...
and fights may disappear and fade...!

So, the rock we have, has many uses you know, but we should use this raw material for good, so humans can develop and grow...!

Without the rock, the atom would not have been split...
And therefore, the fight that exists between nations goes on,

It is constantly louder than the natural bird song...!

For without the rock, the world would be at peace...

And yet, the digging and extracting of rock, only seems to increase...!

It is the rock you know, that has been given, and yet the human mind is nothing but driven...............!

From Rock...

From the shapely female form to other creations from rock! It is not difficult to think of the rock shape opposite as wearing a loose dress by the colours within the natural stone!

Shape, colour and texture bring this sculpture to life and give it movement, dimension and style.

The smoothness of the stone and the hours of work put into creating such a beautiful shape would be many. When one stops and thinks, not one chisel or from a wrongly chipped away piece of rock could be made. The concentration necessary to maintain the regular removal of excess stone would take many hours of work and concentration.

The faces created in the opposite rock formation shows expression and thoughtfulness. To allow the rock the freedom of expression while the shape is created within natural coloured rock formation is breathtaking.

Granite orbs with fine carving and created into water features. The hours of work and carving, chipping away dense rock to form these amazing shapes is almost unbelievable…!

And below, the round grey shapes are complemented by lilac alliums which follow the roundness in shape and form.

The interesting effects of the straight allium stems and the tilting heads of the flowers also add an intererst to the overall display.

The design is clean and fresh with a dramatic play on the colour of the stone, grey and the lilac to lavendar heads of the flower placements.

When one looks deeply into the orbs, we see a whitish hue that shows through the different colours of light-to-dark greys, which have naturally formed over millions of years of naturally occuring rock formations.

James Parker – Sculpture

Using exposed slate as his medium in many of the pieces of sculpture, James, creates mesmerising shapes many resembling the fruit we eat and is often found in the fruit bowl at our homes.

James describes slate '…is a wonderfully versatile material to work with. Nature offers an incredible palette with a plethora of colours and textures, from the heather blues to greys, purples, and greens.'

James enjoys using unrefined materials, such as slate, and then his imagination goes to work in the creations he displays.

Slate being a hardy material, it will not let the gardener down. Because of its endurance, many generations will live to see these outstanding art creations.

James continues, 'Form is an important part of my work. Those which are uncomplicated are often the most satisfying; beautiful in their simplicity'.

As James has said, 'slate offers, texture that many materials do not.' As it can be seen in the bottom tiered sculpture, there are many intricate layers, the lower layer supports the next layer and so on. Each layer in its shape plays its own determining role within the design. He further says, 'The layers create depth, the construction is a source of intrigue to many and the slate sculptures I create, rather than dominate, tend to be dignified within, and communicate with their surroundings.'

Light in the Garden...

The fascination of having lights within our garden displays brings a lot of satisfaction, regardless of the season!

With so many different shapes and colours created within the garden sculptures, it isn't surprising, we become excited at the possibilities and how to use these masterpieces in our own gardens.

From oblong, pinnacles or round shapes, the garden unique decorations, were at Chelsea, in abundance...!

Reflective spheres, turquoise coloured, round shapes placed discretely within the vegetation of a garden can give an enchanting and mystical atmosphere to any night time setting.

From repeated circles of anodized metal, to long sheaves of repeated metal leaf shapes, all are part of the clever shapes of nature.

By repetition of shape, an artist can make many interesting designs come to life. This repetition allows for interest in visual movement and fascination; it plays with our mind, and we want to look for more, this holds visual attraction, and can be somewhat mezmerising...!

I must admit, I do love sweeping lines in sculpture and design; to me, it adds so much more in form than could otherwise be lost had the shape and movement not been introduced at the time of creating the art form.

A Day of Fun...

A young reporter out to get the best shot of the day! Colour and theme were there with personality plus a warmth that made you want to talk to her; she was a delight to have a conversation with.

It's great to see our young people out on a mission and to achieve their goals.

When asking, 'Can I please take your picture?' Her reply, *'Of course you can!'*

Colour, friendship, and a sense of fun cannot be replaced when attending such an event.

The Art of Floristry Design

It takes many years of study to be a competent floral designer. It is not only the use of the physical materials used in flowers, foliage, and assemblages within each created piece of work, but the clever use of rhythm, space, movement, colour, texture, harmony, size of components, construction, balance and alignment, contrast, proportion, and lastly, emphasis, that allows the florist to become the floral artist they become.

The Art of Floristry Design...

Abundance and celebration are the only categories we can describe the flower designs at this year's show.

From the Hogarth Curve seen in the opposite photograph using contrasting colours of different tonal values of whites and creams to lavender and purples, with a slight intermission of straw stalks.

To create the Hogarth Curve, one needs to have a firm background in fixed mass floral design and the experience of the artist is seen by the construction and placements within the work. A pleasure and delight to see.

Opposite, the contrasting colours of lemon to yellow and then pinks to lavenders in the two designs opposite is again seen in the Hogarth Curve shapes.

The shapes, not clearly seen in the photograph, are a combination of a pair of reflecting shapes is both visually pleasing and creative.

The unique combination of four designs to form one design, rightfully so, wins a Silver Medal.

Opposite, with so much emphasis on renewable and recycling, this drum has been put to good use.

The hydrangea is an old-fashioned flower and is greatly appreciated by most floral artists, whether working within the commercial floristry industry, or in the local floral art clubs and organisations.

With colour blocking now seen in many floral designs, it's a relief from the coloured speckling that used to be so popular.

By mass colour-blocking, we not only enhance the floral designs, but add visual impact to each design we create.

Opposite, the vibrancy of colour and creativity are not readily seen within any photograph. The mass effect of the flowers in oranges, pinks, and reds with gushing Cymbidium orchids from within the design, and then tying the work together is a bendable red tube.

There are many beautiful flowers within the design; at the lower end, towards the base of the arrangement, are purple dendrobium orchids, salmon-coloured roses, and occasionally seen are strelitzia flowers.

Giving the design an almost semi-industrial appearance, a piece of scaffolding; by adding the scaffolding, the shapes are harsh in appearance when compared to the delicate and almost whimsical appearance of the flowers, and the supporting leaves that, not only break up the flower colour but also the flower shape, texture, and appearance!

The mixing of hard rustic rock also seems to stabilise the overall impact.

Below, the use of colour, texture and movement encapsulate the visual impact of the presentation.

This 'Gold' winning arrangement, titled 'Botanical Spillage' has cascading flowers and foliage making this design sing. The weeping green Amaranthus, striking oranges, purples and lavenders are blended in this mass vertical design giving a sense of mass and abundance.

Purple alliums, sweeping tendrils of unopened orchid spikes, and a mass of different coloured orange flowers, including double-parrot tulips, are pushed together to make this splendid mass display. It was nice to see plumosus asparagus fern being used in the 21st Century; it was a fern that lost popularity several years ago; it gives a lightness, airy and ethereal presence to many flower and wedding designs.

Please keep in mind, asparagus may be toxic to cats.

Below, a framework of cane supports this arrangement of mixed and different foliage with a mixture of perfectly placed light field flowers; this blend makes this design delightful and a pleasure to see.

With a combination of different whites, to cream, apricots, and

different tonal values within the lavenders to purple hues, and the added textural value of small alliums, all make this a soft and tranquil design that is very pleasing to study and learn from.

The void towards the centre of the design helps to keep the soft and dignified appearance of the completed work.

Opposite, the 'magic of the moment' was caught in this amazing, traditional mass design.

Leaving the viewer with the 'Wow...', '...*please show me some more...!*' feeling, it was the essence of the show this year: abundance, but not extravagant or garish, but fun and colour.

From massed delphinium flower heads in soft, and blushing pinks, to larkspur and dusky-pink roses, all used in blocked colouring; blocking adds to the impact of any design whether large or small...

Lavender alliums, white larkspur, purple Easter daisy, and the newness of young summer green foliage all add to a majestic and impacting display in the traditional massed design.

The anchor the work, again, an old metal drum has been repurposed, painted black and used as the container. The design leaves a positive and pleasing impression with the viewer.

Moving away from the colours of purple and pinks, opposite, it was inspirational to see whites and creams brought together, these colours being interspersed with apricots and oranges.

The anchoring down of the woven basket shaped container, helps to bring about the overall pleasing appearance of the arrangement.

With cascades of flowing white phalaenopsis orchids, white allium, and what appears to be long rolls of natural cotton, white arum lilies and again, plumosus asparagus fern being used.

The sheer abundance of the design is breathtaking and interesting to see. The movement of texture, colour, form, and expression are all about the working components within the design.

Gloriosa lilies also play their part in demanding to be noticed in the vibrancy of the orange colours seen.

Opposite, a very different approach from the traditional massed flower arrangement was used in this design.

The centre of the design gives the appearance of pink coral and hints of the world's oceans and yet, the abundance of moss with pairs of egg placements, suggests the beginning of new life.

Dashes of yellow also add an interest, while the circles seem to resemble the world going through its different motions.

The rocks to the left edge also play a role in adding different colour and texture to the design.

The eye is drawn to the centre, coral-pink placement, which again could suggest the sea and the start of all life from the very beginning.

This was an interesting and very different approach to interpretive floral design and work.

Opposite, the magic of the semi-circle in floristry design. Circles, semi-circles, and the use of curves in any floral arrangement always adds a touch of mysticism to the creation.

Unlike many other mediums used in

the creative arts such as clay, paint, marble, metals, and other materials, 'flowers are of the moment...' Once their beauty has faded, they are no longer of the moment...!

It is this intangible aspect of flower design and arranging flowers by the floral artist that keeps the floral artist's interest. It is the challenge as they strive for new and different designs to create, and different flowers and foliage to use; their determination to create something beautiful that can never be created a second time, regardless of how the artist will try.

I have tried many times to re-create a floral design and regardless of how hard I have tried; it cannot be done. Something similar will emerge, but it will not be identical!

When looking through the floral archway corridor in the above, one cannot help but think of perhaps, taking off the walking shoes, and skipping through the floral display. An abundance of colour, movement and creativity is used in this spectacular design.

Opposite, and below, is a 'Gold' winning design, titled, 'The Beauty of Recycling,' is of lilacs, lavender and purple, with just a touch of chartreuse; thus, a combination of peace and stillness with using colour! With so many of the cut flowers sitting in singular bottles, the design will remain fresh for many days; this is a new approach to floristry.

With two tiers adding to the mix of the design giving a view of abundance, harmony, and dance. The use of moss adds in the grounding necessary to let the viewers know that the flowers are growing; they are fresh and have life within their form.

We are now seeing recycled bottles and many other recyclable objects being brought into 21st Century floristry, surely, this identifies the concerns of waste products, land and sea fill that are prevalent within our world environment!

Even in a busy flower show, I have found, within these colour combinations, the peace that is given to my brain, through visual satisfaction, is extraordinary.

Below is a combination of pleasing satisfaction.

When one takes the time to look, study and identify, there are swirls within the placements of flowers, cane, and foliage. Each placement leans to the left of the design, with the cane leading the visual way through the arrangement.

Vines, moss, and cane are integral to the flow of the design. The solid shape and placement of columns of

stocks in white and pink, and the blue delphinium, white allium, and the splendid colour of rose-coloured peony flowers, all make for an interesting combination within the visual experience.

The strength of the blocking of the green delphinium foliage gives a nice transition to the mossy base.

Like all floral designs shown, each one is an expression of the creator! Below, this 'Gold' winning design, titled, 'On The Verge,' has tall, elegant placements which add the necessary height to incorporate the lamppost, which is an accessory to the overall design.

The autumn colours incorporated in the lower placements add to the depth of creativity.

When the human mind wants to create, the work we create can both astonish and please all who are blessed to see it.

'Magnificent,' were the words I used when I first saw this wonderful, massed work. From the 'eye-catching' moment of seeing the double fern-leaf peony, the raffia wrapped twine threading its way through the design, and then looking deeply to the smaller placements of lavender to purple flowers, and again the use of the Hogarth Curve in the flowing lines; the overall combination was breathtaking.

When such magnificent blooms as the peony is grown to capture the visual impact of the spectator, we know within our hearts, that someone, somewhere, has worked very hard.

The appearance of a clock face on the different ends of sawn wood, help in the fun of the moment in the design. There are no sombre moments, just a time to look and enjoy the pleasure of the beauty before you.

The Magnificence of The Peony...

Floristry and Floral Art

Elegance and structure help to bring about this beautiful Ikebana design.

As part of my own journey into design, I spent a year attending weekly classes with an Ikebana Master artist in Australia. It was a beautiful time used in total creation and the absorption of the positive use of line, space, movement, and materials.

Each movement has meaning including earth, water, and sky.

The use of the new shoots within the maple branch placements, the strength of the line from what may be a gladiolus, sword shaped leaf, the use of a full flower iris and the iris buds, with a placement of hydrangea stem complete with new buds and fresh leaves, then the placement of one yellow wildflower daisy all adds to the rhythm of this design.

The Florist

Not knowing what to do, the time had come, to leave school and look for a trade and start the new…!

With no decisions formed, the mind was empty, and age did not understand, for if not a career chosen, the future will obscure from view…!

Urgency was emphasized and plans all set, an interview was made, 'But your parents' must attend' I was told…!

Not knowing what to expect, the interview over and new trade begun, and to begin, it was not much fun…!

Hard days were earnt, small wages were received; from thinking now… It was only three pounds a week and not a lot could be done…!

But learning was the 'call of the day,' for they had much to give, and much to say…!

Constance Spry, was a name often heard, and my teachers were brought in, for they were teachers of much renown…!

For hours were spent doing and learning, but filled with 'in-between time' were hard and cold, so much to do, long hours were spent…

Mossing wire frames, for many unnamed – funerals, I learnt a lot, dead people were a daily mention: work hard and do not relent…!

For this was an investment into the future and time well spent…!

Cold winter mornings, Christmas is near, holly wreaths to make, displays filled with ice, for this time was cold and not nice…!

Spring would come and daffodils appear, how lovely to see the bright smiling faces, and the very good cheer…!

Those sunny days of learning, the art, and the skill…, for those days have stood well with me, and I learnt to the fill…!

For the question I constantly asked of my mind: 'Why do people buy flowers…?'

For onto university, I needed to ask, which allowed me to research and discover for hours and hours…!

The reason people buy flowers is an emotional need...!
A sense of expression, a sense of happiness, of love, of sadness they may feel...!

And so it is, the florist's role, is not only about, beauty and creation...!

But about the need to give to another... And the need to give to that individual soul...!

Opposite, this is not necessarily a flower arrangement, but it has a combination of elements that may allow it to fit into this position. Cool, refreshing and the use of foliage to create the feeling that you are within the rain forest of some magical land.

Interspersed within the green plant placements are small touches of the orange colour gloriosa lily and just at times a touch of white is added…!

The grey square frame that acts as the boundaries within the design are strong in appearance when contrasted with the delicate placements of leaf and flower materials.

And then, the water is added to the base of the design supporting the resemblance to a rain forest of South America, some parts of Asia and of course, to Northern Australia, and other related areas that encourage natural growth in safe and clean environments.

The use of different mosses and occasionally the use of pink fungi, make this a masterful design.

The Mush Room

Mushrooms, mushrooms, mushrooms, what else is needed?

With so many, now edible varieties being produced, mushrooms not only look wonderful in many culinary delights, but they are good for the human body, and brain when incorporated into our everyday diet.

There are many benefits to the human body when mushrooms are in the food we eat. Mushrooms contain Riboflavin, which is good for our blood cell production, they also contain many of the B vitamins including niacin and pantothenic acid which help to support and protect the heart. Niacin helps to support our digestive systems and keeping our skin healthy.

Mushrooms also contain antioxidants which help to eliminate cancer.

The Mush Room...

To say the minimum would not be enough. To at first see this stand with such a variety of different shaped and coloured mushrooms, was intriguing. The shapes, some of which, look like sculptures, were so different.

The natural development of nature's own artistic structures in the Design Elements have been used to the maximum extent.

The use of shape, colour, impact was at natures beck-and-call as the natural form of the mushrooms grew into shape.

From soft-rose pinks, to lemons, white, cream and more. Of course, not forgetting the familiar browns of the species.

Enhancing the shapes through tasteful and singular white stands, all of which mimicked the underside of many different groups of mushrooms.

Opposite, this lemon oyster mushroom was outstanding as it stood in the display. The top of the traditional shaped mushroom, which most of us would be familiar with, is smooth, with the undulation seen on the underside! This mushroom is similar in appearance.

Not only do mushrooms offer many health benefits, but they can distinguish many culinary dishes which may be seen in restaurants and other good food outlets.

From lemons to the more familiar browns, (below). often seen in our supermarkets. These however, do look appear to grow from one solid-central structure, which may be wood or a moss-type base.

With so many mushrooms in the natural world, without the cultivated types now being developed, we may see an explosion of colours and shapes in the future.

Shapes, Colour & Texture

The word 'Fascination...' comes to mind when we took the time to look closely at these different species of mushrooms.

Each display makes a talking point, and each has its own story to tell.

Caley Bros are taking the mushroom to new and enviable heights in the array of gourmet and medicinal, home-grown mushrooms.

All the mushroom displays sit on paper plinths. For growing nutrition of the plants, Caley Bros use coffee grounds, sawdust, soy hulls and old books. All are grown from waste products and can be readily grown at home.

Garden Displays

People love to look and experience the garden displays at the Chelsea Flower Show. People are given inspiration to work within their own gardens through the cleverness of the designs on display.

The incorporation of charity stands, and the good work that small groups within our communities are creating in allotments, small gardens, all of which are acting to bring people together. This may not have happened, if the idea for community involvement had not happened in the first place.

Show Gardens

With many gardens to visit and to board the plane the next day back to Australia, it literally became scarce moments spent at each display. Having said that, we did manage to see everything that was of great interest to us.

The gardens at the show are always incredibly exciting and full of new ideas.

The Royal Entomological Society Garden opposite created a semi-dome of recycled steel and hexagonal glazing panels. The interior links a screen to microscopes which in turn provides a study space. With a direct purpose for study, the coloured glass, colours radiated from the sunlight, are a similar replica to the eye of an insect. This display was a fascination in construction and the use of materials for the study of insects.

The biodiverse planting attracts insects to the natural habitat created, thus, allowing them to pollinate and provide a year-round food supply and the follow-up interest of study.

Not seen, a flowing stream, and still pool, allows for the collection of water which supports a variety of insect life.

52

Titled, 'A Letter from a Million Years Past...'

This garden allows a little insight into how medicinal herbs grow and are harvested on Jirisan, the highest mountain on mainland Korea.

The open top of the building, seen in the larger photograph, herbs, once picked, this area is used for drying the herbs.

The creating of sustainable landscapes and environments, by Jihae Hwang, are viewed from a conceptual viewpoint, whilst having many ancient roots in practise and use. It is the environment and the use of natural materials that allows us to see this insight into the knowledge and understanding of how herbs grow and can be used to assist human health.

Having said that, it is not surprising to see this garden design and its message taken to the Chelsea Flower Show.

The use of natural, but muted colours, are part of the natural world, often with colour only coming into play at the right seasonal time of the year; such a time is dedicated to the plants or animals of that environment.

Many builders and building designers are slowly turning to natural earth products to build sustainable and thermally efficient homes which cut down on energy for heating and lighting, which in turn, supports the earth and the environment!

Coolness of Colour...
The Myeloma Garden

How many hues, tints, and shades of green are there in the natural world of vegetation?

It would be impossible to imagine the world without the colour green, and yet, somehow, when we are so very busy, we can miss this treasure.

Natural living green gives off extraordinary energy that supports health and wellbeing for all living things, including animals, insects, and human beings...!

As with all of nature's treasures, we should each enjoy the moments of these visual sensations.

Many people diagnosed with life threatening illnesses find a sanctuary in the garden, and so it is that Chris Bradshaw, has designed this festival of green representing The Myeloma Charity, United Kingdom.

Here we see seven, or maybe more green colours, which are interspersed with a touch of white and small splashes of blue...! When looking at the display, the feeling of tranquillity, peace and breathless sensation can overcome you as the colours throw their beauty out to their spectators.

The ferns are particularly interesting in their visual presentation, with light and shade playing its role as the different colours of the clouds above show the feather-like fronds, against the wider solid leaves seen opposite and below.

Just to throw our visual senses into disarray, the slight colouring of reddish-to-orange shows itself in the larger leaves seen in the photographs.

The Natural Affinity Garden

The coolness of this garden with the intermingling of some grey-green foliage, touches of Wedgewood blue, and the occasional whisp of white flowers leave an impression of coolness and charm; it is unequivocally, the coolness and softness of the traditional English garden.

This garden is composed of three main elements: trees, plants, and stone within three specific zones.

The plants have been specifically selected for the sensory qualities within each garden zone.

The zones are designed to stimulate the visitor's senses, and this supports the nurturing of individual wellbeing.

The garden design by Camellia Taylor, gives the visitor an insight

into how each of us rely on our senses to help us work, play, have time out and a time for relaxation.

As a teacher of psychology and having taught many different children and young adults with different needs, when understanding that our senses play major roles in our lives, it is the acknowledgement of the senses, that assists us to effectively manage different life situations.

In the photograph opposite, it is the soft touch of pink that shows the feeling of gentleness and ease of the plant placement.

The design is an acknowledgement to Aspens, the charity that provides quality care and support for people on the autism spectrum, and those with learning disabilities. The team at Aspens work to support, not only the young person but their families.

Aspens provides a rich environment that allows positive learning and growth, developing maturity and to increase each person's enrichment enabling them to take opportunities, as they increase, in their knowledge and wellbeing.

While the garden is full of sensory stimulation, the one element that allows for the grounding of the design are the rocks seen in the below photograph.

By introducing this stabilisation element, the rocks allow us to take visual time out and to mentally rest on the journey.

Proportionally, it is difficult to understand visual balance when in the creation stages of any design. Once construction is completed, it is only possible to see if the design has the visual balance necessary to make it acceptable and pleasing to the human eye.

This design was both extremely rewarding to look at, and most definitely added to our satisfaction of the day.

Turning Rubbish to Treasure

Recycle, reuse, and help to save the planet and the global environment.

Whilst we have gone through the Industrial Revolution, and many have benefited from the outcomes of the inventions of the time, it is time now to 'take stock' of the outcomes.

Recycling and reuse were very much the theme of the show. Not forgetting the other positive outcomes for our natural world insects, animals, and flora. By recycling, we will start in the beginning phases of

allowing the planet to start to heal.

Having said that, in so many parts of the world, there are more homeless people, and they all need shelter.

This design was an interesting concept that left us thinking, 'how can we in Australia and the United Kingdom, use more items to recycle them and use them in garden features? It is only a small step at this point, but something we all need to think about when thinking, 'we need a new shed…!' Or when something needs replacing in the garden such as garden furniture and other replacement items.

The pinnacle on the roof of this garden building was more a study in the use of different materials used to create interest within a garden setting…

The sloping roof structure had a mesh-type construction, with what appeared to be dried laurel leaves attached replacing either shingles or slate.

Many dried leaves such as magnolia, and some laurels, give the appearance of softly polished leather once they have been preserved in glycerine. The leaves could be misleading and may be cut from a form of metal. Regardless of the material used, it does show that many items can be recycled and used in garden constructions.

The interest in the roof design does not stop there, but looking deeper, one needs to follow the shape of curved pipes, possibly resembling growing vine stems, these may have been re-purposed to collect rainwater.

Such a garden building may become a place of relaxation and enjoyment.

Gracious and Cool...

As the warm afternoon sun hit the show, the tantalising coolness of this display was felt by many visitors.

We naturally realise that mosses are cool, but when seen within the context of a warm day, it does something to our minds, it seems almost out of character with the Centre of London location!

In this design, many different mosses were used to cover rocks and to give the feeling of an ancient landscape.

As singular cell plants, mosses offer an added advantage to the planet in the absorption of CO_2, while offering in return, clean air which enables all living creatures to survive.

With such an emphasis on natural and back to nature, and the natural environment, it takes us many light years away from the finely clipped lawns and the gardens of the sixties, seventies, and eighties...!

Daisies, Daisies, Daisies...

The singular beauty of a daisy patch in any garden conjures up the idea of a daisy circle in any person's mind, relates to fairies at the bottom of the garden, wishing wells and buttercups. And so, it is with natural wildflower gardens.

Sleepy sunny, summer afternoons and all the feeling of lazy days were present in this garden display. It presents stillness, sunshine, and a time to doze....!

A natural selection of summer flowers is easy to accept with the hustle and bustle of a busy show...

More Choices for Cost-Effective Garden Designs

With such a choice of design, and the use of many different building materials, it allows the human mind to go crazy. Used in the below design are concrete containers which give a strength to any garden display. Now, there are available, environmentally friendly concretes that are made from re-cycled materials. They leave no carbon footprint and make for healthy environments for both humans and animals.

The curved archway in the background allows us to look further and beyond the display. This is an interesting concept as it allows the garden to extend beyond its physical boundaries!

By using a bit of creative imagination, we can make even the most boring of backgrounds look interesting.

Imagine an old, shed wall that has been annoying since the house was bought, or since the house was renovated! Don't let those bricks go to waste, use them to make a feature in the garden…!

Or if there is somebody selling off wood end leftovers, all can

contribute to 1, saving money, and 2, creating a tranquil and positive extra living space…!

Recycling and maximising used materials will all help in reducing waste, pollution, and the stress on the earth's wellbeing.

Opposite, the visual play of the wood cuts left in their natural state glued against a deep-slate coloured wall, create an exceptional, extra living space, and contribute to an individual 'peace of mind'.

The Platform Garden, can give many ideas for revamping an old garden shed, wall, or simply create a space that you can use in different ways. Once making your decision the outcomes can be miraculous…!

In the opposite photograph, green tiles, which I remember being on the walls of the underground tube in London, when I was a child, are now a fashion statement. Green is traditionally recognised as a growth colour, so for the 21st Century, it is visually, very acceptable.

In this setting, and as you can see, the ground covering is cement, but if planter tubs are placed strategically, even unsightly surfaces can become glamorous and inviting…!

Opposite, large beams of wood created into an 'open air' outside room, can make an extraordinarily inviting back garden room which can be perfect for 'working from home' on a summer afternoon or while taking a tea or coffee break.

So many more liveable outside spaces are being produced by people being creative for either found or re-cycled materials.

The Magic of Space...

We had this little space you see – wasted it was, untidy too...!
something needed to be done and start from new...!

For much space we needed to have more fun –
books to read, articles to write and so much to be done,
without the traditional fight and created from none...
!
'You've taken my space...', we could hear them scream,
'You're just awful, I was sitting there...' and

So, it went on into the night....!
The yells and the screams and into the fight...!

At last peace, descends, the space was now clear...
we can sit and listen and now at least hear...!

For space is a premium, I can hear you all cheer...!
'Yes, in our house too, and only meant for just the few...!'

Sometimes, it's nice to sit and lament...
for precious times that are often spent...!

Crowds are more and people are many...
and so, it is, life's special times are forgotten,
if not given space or any...!

Life quickly passes, for that we all know...
and it's the time we need to go and to show...!

Experiences are plenty and good to recall, and it's,
the mind space needed, when into the fall...!

Heartaches come and endurance is needed,
for time will not tolerate if not heard the call...!

It is in the 'Magic of Space' that songs and books are written...
For the special times we wonder, we fall and are smitten....!

And so, the 'Magic of space' is often so rare, but the mind is always
working to find the space there...!

The Great Pavilion

Chelsea is a wonderful show case for spectators to see how different community groups are working together to create support and good for the society, and in turn, many people.

The Great Pavilion provides some marvellous insights into the world of horticulture, community togetherness and a mass of creative living colour that team-ship, when more than one mind, hard work and planning can achieve.

I have written much on how our great human minds are always up 'for the challenge' to create something different, something that leaves a lingering and lasting impression on others, and this show does just that in the Great Pavilion.

Expectations...

The Great Pavilion offers such a magnitude of surprises, it is always a highlight on the trip. Upon seeing for the first time, the green display below, offered solace and coolness to the visual senses on a warm, beautiful, early, English spring day.

The coolness offered is immediately felt, with many visitors stopping to take in the magnificence of the display.

The photograph does not do the depth, and the feeling the creative intelligence used, to bring the combination of living plants and static rocks together, justice.

The use of ancient ferns, so vital to the environment in this time of global warming, brings us again to the mosses that help to support and maintain a constant in, and stable healthy plant and animal existence, are all seen in this one display.

And, of course, it won a 'Gold' at the show...!

Upside-Down Flowers…!
The Yellow Brick Road…

How fascinating, such imagination…! Flowers hanging upside down and all looking as cheeky as ever…! The Yellow Brick Road, of course the name is taken from the film, Wizard of Oz.

This display by John Cullen, creates the world of magic and takes us into another dimension of interpretive design.

People stopped, laughed, pointed as they took the visual display back to their own memories of the film; such a clever way to bring a special day to the visitors, some of which, like us, had travelled thousands of miles to see such outstanding creations.

And from another angle, the Yellow Brick Road is clearly seen. Masses of flowers create this display with separate group placements of white alliums, which seem to appear in many displays this year.

Masses of achillea, 'Moon Dust' giving the yellowish to green overtone within the design.

Some achilleas, when in the budding stage, have a young greyish leaf and bud before the flowers and leaves mature into open

flowers. This aspect of the flower's growth can give a mist or ghostly appearance, which is fascinating to see as it blends into the overall design.

Different angles to the work give a perfect opportunity to see how magical the yellow brick road really is...!

Soft and Demure...

To blend soft pastel colours within any garden setting allows our minds to wonder, and goodness, in the times we are living through with wars, negative media, and so many people of the world wondering, 'what is held in the future for them and their families?' It's at these times, we all need some light mental relief.

A place to sit, look and marvel at the many flowers that are now in this 21st Century, and how many, if not millions of years, has it taken for us to look and wonder at these original and natural wonders that nature provides...?

Without too much thought, we can enjoy our natural wildflowers

and cherish the seasons that bring forth the spectacles each year, such is the enchantment of the natural world.

Soft blending of colour, while allowing the natural formation of the foliage to have a voice, were all part of the appeal to this natural garden design.

Cor-ten – Popular and Different...

Weathering steel is seen on many newly erected buildings in both Australia and the United Kingdom.

In this display by the Birmingham City Council, and within its 'Free Parks for the People,' shows off the creativity of using an industrial steel material, such as Cor-ten in creative design.

There are the large tulips seen in the above picture, but when looking closer, there are three young characters pushing a hand-pushed lawnmower, and then looking even deeper there are cut from cor-ten, foxes playing within the flower beds.

Another of the features of this display include a large lily-shape flower which appears to be made from either platted cor-ten strands or from a hefty, dried vine of the same colour.

The abundance of colour allows the happiness of the event to come through and touch our feelings and emotions.

With so much to see and so much going on in such small surroundings, it's easy to forget about any concerns or problems we may have had!

It is not only the busyness of the event, but the effective use of space is remarkable. Just to stop and think, prior to about three weeks before the event opens, the grounds in front of The Royal Chelsea Hospital lovely down to lawns and flower borders. Within about a three-week period, the Chelsea Flower Show and its exhibits are slowly brought together.

The ground is dug, soil and lawns are removed, with all the exhibits in place, the show begins, and what a spectacle it is each year.

No two years have ever been the same, with new ideas for displays, different varieties of plants of all types and new flower types take their place at their display stands. And so it is, new materials are introduced, such as cor-ten, a commercial building product, that is now part of the garden and display scene.

The blending of the harsh steel with the delicate flowers on display, is almost in conflict but that too is what creative art is about. It is about

using the ordinary to make the extraordinary, and by doing this, we can see how so many more materials can be used tastefully, and effectively, in garden, parks and large public areas.

Cor-ten is a sustainable material that allows rust to build on the exposed areas to the environment, the rust then acts as a protective coating to the steel.

The use of abundance and imagination helps to make the Birmingham City Council display as delightful as it was in 2022.

Alliums Galore...

To see the natural height of these magnificent plants, is itself pleasing but to see them in such quantities is nothing more than resplendent of the perseverance to develop beautiful flower specimens.

The looped stem and bud of the allium is novel and eye catching as seen in the side and lower photograph.

Alliums are a wonderful addition to the flower industry and the scope they offer in both traditional and modern flower arrangements.

These majestic and sculptured flower heads offer such an interest to the viewer and yet, they may hold the mystery of their own story!

Amaryllis Lilies

Amaryllis lilies were much admired by the Greeks and the flowers are mentioned in their mythology.

Going back to those ancient times, one can only again, be impressed, as the Greek population would have been at the delightful and sculptured shapes, the clearness of the colours and the lasting impression these flowers leave on our memories and emotions.

With their distinctive colours, the amaryllis lily is a popular garden and gift plant.

The plant is often associated with determination, love, and beauty.

Whilst amaryllis are often thought of as red, there are many other colours to choose from, and to melt our hearts.

These plants are often given as gifts or presents and symbolise to many people, new beginnings, which may reflect hard work and the determination to succeed with a chosen goal or achievement.

As a decorative flower, when teamed with alliums, they make striking modern flower arrangements that all people can achieve.

Surprisingly, the amaryllis lily is a distant relative to the asparagus family. The plant also has many health benefits including, it has anti-inflammatory benefits that reduce inflammation and ease body pain, it has antimicrobial properties, and has been used to heal wounds, cuts, and abrasions.

With so much to offer from the natural world, the amaryllis will be high on our shopping list for future gift buying.

Roses, Roses, Roses...

The beautiful rose blooms produced by the David Austin Nursery, never cease to impress the audience and spectators of the Show.

From stunning white to apricot and a great variety of pink blooms show us the achievement and beauty that can be achieved by perseverance and the love of the flowers.

To reach the pinnacles of perfection that was shown at this year's show can only leave the viewer feeling mentally replenished at seeing such a spectacle of achievement.

The perfume from the display was heaven sent and to say the least, it was an exquisite experience for just a few moments while enjoying the abundance of colour and headiness of the moment.

From single blooms to masses of showing combinations of colour, all was there for the audience to see and enjoy.

Roses have an ancient history and the love by all civilisations and generations who have had the pleasure of their beauty, never fades.

And so it was with this year's show of roses, colours, perfume, abundance and all of the ingredients that make the Show, the Show...!

Big Show – 'GOLD' Disbud Chrysanthemums

And what a Show…? Such magnificent blooms and the white were breathtaking at the first glance.

Of course, a Gold Award was deserved by such a magnificent show of these blooms.

These are again, an ancient bloom and kept in the gaze of the public by the enthusiasm of the growers and nurseries that cultivate and give us this visual feast.

The chrysanthemum was originally cultivated in China in the 15th Century BC.

Originally, being within the herb family, it was used for its medicinal purposes.

By 1630 AD 500 cultivars had been recorded. In 2014, it was estimated that there were up to or more than 20,000 cultivars throughout the world, with up to 7,000 in China.

Chrysanthemums have a royal attachment and are part of the Imperial Seal of Japan.

This magnificent flower is traditionally an autumn flower and associated with many ancient festivals in Japan. In Japanese culture, the bloom has its own symbolic day known as Chrysanthemum Day. There are several ancient festivals in autumn related to the bloom included the sacred festivals, one of which is held on the 9th day of the 9th month. This date coincides with the first day the Imperial Court held the first

Daffodils & Narcissus – A Sign of Spring...

Many people worldwide love daffodils or narcissus, they are indeed a beautiful flower in the springtime. Their colours are pure, perfume heavenly and the shape and texture of each bloom is crisp, sharp, and definite.

The people of the United Kingdom also love their daffodils, but they are native to Europe, the Middle East, and Africa.

The ancient Greeks also loved their daffodils and had the belief they brought good luck and joy; they too, used daffodils for home decoration, and adornment in the temples.

Daffodils are not an edible flower; they carry toxins in the yellow trumpet, petals, and bulbs; all parts of the plant have toxins.

The daffodil originated from the amaryllis lily.

Due to their popularity daffodils now come in a wide range of size, colour, and shapes.

Many of the old-fashioned daffodils had strong fragrances, and some are still enjoyed today; these include,
'Golden Spur,' 'Pheasant's Eye' and 'Early Louisiana.'

Clematis – Pictures Of Perfection...

Could there be anything more beautiful than the sun-kissed clematis on an early summer morning or when the dew has left its silver bubble to reflect the beauty of each single flower?

And so it is, and yet, another piece of nature's perfect creations.

Now, clematis comes in a range of different colours, to which all our different senses react.

From purples to vivid pinks, white, cream and back again to different hues of magenta.

Some of the clematis are scented, mainly in the climbing varieties. The deeply coloured purple clematis has a scent often released on a late summer afternoon when there is a degree of humidity in the air.

Scent differs between varieties, but Betty Corning is well known for the scent it has.

From miniature varieties to the larger flowers, all of which are stunningly beautiful.

From gentle, soft petal shapes to the intrinsically sophisticated centre of the flower, all of which add to the spectacle on display.

When the flowers are seen in mass proportions, it allows us to see the complexity and profusion of the creations.

With decadence of colour, perfume and excitement fills the air as these splendid specimens create their own majestic environment.

With numbers of people wanting to see these flowers and their plants, we were fortunate to capture these moments of splendour.

Picture of Perfection...

These displays will play with our memories for many years to come. The perfume will linger, and the thoughts will return….!

Clematis

The Night...

The evening scent fills the air, for flowers are letting you know they are there...!

Insects and night birds are waiting for the feast to begin, pollen and nectar to make their hearts sing....!

Flowers that thrive in the night, they are there and without any fright...!

Lavender, purple, pink, and white you may see...!
For the moonlight shines and twinkles on glistening petals
and flowers that are free...

Before the visitors start to arrive, first a late-night flying bee on his way home to the hive –
he stops for a feast and then on his journey, he goes on to strive....!

If you wait long enough you might see, late arrivals...
Such as the moth and firefly all wanting to find nectar and food to help them survive....!

The night swift may occasionally arrive, for it's the flowers high in the trees that are easier to find...

This allows them to feed with all who are kind....

And for many, they are safe in the trees, like bats who only feast at night, for all are needed and all need to eat without any fight....!

And so, it is, the night may be busier than the day, four our animals and insects we owe a great deal...!

Leave pesticides and chemicals out of the gardens and out of land fill...!

For once the creatures mentioned above, have little resistance to the fatal chemicals that make them ill, and many will not survive –
even if they are given a pill...!!!

Succulents and Cacti

Some people love them and some not so...!

I must admit, it has taken me many years to like these plants. I think the reason being, there are so many different and colourful types now, that they may even fit into the 'Cute' category of plants.

Most definitely, when these little gems start to show their flowers at different times of the year, they are very pleasing to have as indoor plants.

While in my training in floristry, one of my principal jobs was to look after the cacti...!

After their careful nurturing, I would spend the next week taking the small, barb-like hairs from my very sore fingers! Only to start the following week doing the same job...!

From those beginnings, the cacti and succulent families have come a long way. Now, such decorative plants, they make a talking point in many venues.

Showing so much colour, combinations, and difference, it is no wonder that people are now seeing these plants through different eyes.

The mesmerising balls of cotton wool opposite, would make an interesting focal point in a large modern home where the full complexity of their different beauty can be appreciated.

The appreciation of the succulent and cacti form, shape, texture, and the visual movement from one part of the plant to another, is, a study in time and patience.

A beautiful combination of plants made the spectacular displays this year.

The Magic of the Moment...

Combinations of texture, colour and movement can stop us in our tracks and this magical combination did just that. Here we see the different textures, amazing colours and plant shapes all playing a part in the different plantings within each display.

With rounded to spear-shapes, the different colours, and succulent types, these all work together to bring such visual delight to the array of plants now available.

Not only are there varied plants but succulents have the added advantage of giving unique and different types of flower displays at different times of the year.

Many succulents are affordable to begin collecting and seem to double up as they grow giving an abundance of colour, shape, and pleasure.

Many old containers that may collecting dust or put into the recycle bin for later use, can be used to make stunning indoor gardens that can be delightful all year round.

From many golden yellow colours to crimsons, whites and creams, these little gems can produce interesting displays.

In writing this information, I cannot forget to mention, it is the repetition of shape in many succulents that makes the plants so interesting to look at.

The display above and below allows us to see how the floret shape is repeated and repeated in the many individual potted plants seen.

The greyish plants can give an almost ghostly look, but when combining the plants together with other house plants, the interest they produce can be fascinating. If combining a grey coloured succulent with a pink cyclamen plant the textures, colour and shapes are splendid.

When a mass of cacti or succulents are seen in one space, the plants not only look spectacular, but they become a feast to see and study.

Watching the plants grow and enjoy their environment is not only good for them, but also good for us. We learn to stop, take a breath, and enjoy the time spent.

Plants in themselves are a therapy and help us slow down, take a moment, all of which help us towards good health and wellbeing.

Masses of shape, form, colour, and plants support the indulgence we see on these pages.

Semi-Tropical Flowers

I don't know if other florists or flower arrangers feel like I do, when I see a display such as the tropical flowers, interspersed with a few nerines, and other showy blooms, it makes me feel, *'I would love to have my secateurs with me now, I know I could do some magnificent floral displays...!'* However, that is not the reason we are attending this amazing show.

Jacques Amand has used delightful hot pinks of the ginger flowers through to flaming oranges and reds. Pulling the combination of colour and balance together, we see the leaves of the liquid amber in the photographs.

The magnificent leaves of the caladium plant, though a very large leaf combination is seen here, the size and colour of the leaves help to give visual strength, while picking up the hot pink tones of the nerines and ginger plants.

White allium towards the back of the design allows our eyes to travel slowly, without jolts, over such a striking combination and profusion of colour, texture, and magnificence.

Most leaf shapes are flat and therefore, make a positive contribution to flower design as most flowers are three dimensional and have a petal formation. By combining the different dimensions, and plains which allows the eye to easily move from one point of interest to another.

Positive leaf placements, allow floral design to become interesting and allows the viewer to become involved within the creation.

Below, the display presented by the Trinidad and Tobago delegation have created a beautiful and fascinating exhibit, showing different native flowers, vegetables and trees that grow on the islands.

Full use was made of the living materials used in the presentation with vibrancy, excitement, movement, and fascination built into the exhibit.

When we look at the different textures, shapes, vibrancy of the material used, it shows the commitment to giving the spectators a stunning and memorable experience.

Remembering all that is seen, with the worldwide expertise and competition shown by all exhibitors, this display has left its mark as a show piece.

Within tropical plant material, there are a great deal of different shapes and a serenade of colours not always seen in the traditional of Northern Hemisphere floral and leaf material.

Ginger flowers, anthuriums, variegated foliage are all part of the cacophony of colour, shape, movement, excitement, and positive energy seen in these designs.

From falling and trailing vines, to vertical and straight, upward sweeping leaves, ferns, cascading throngs of orchids in upward spiralling movement all the design a poetry in motion of flowering plants and cut flowers.

Trinidad and Tobago

Masses of colour, vibrance and energy are seen in the Trinidad and Tobago floral exhibits.

Zantedeschia – Colours to Make Your Heart Sing...

Such amazing flowers, especially, when seen in great abundance as at the show.

The colours are sharp, but it is the shape of the flower that lends itself to modern and traditional flower arranging and in bridal work.

In bridal work, the stems can be left in length for a modern approach to wedding design, or they can be wired into place.

From a sharp sherbet-lemon colour to muted purple-to-lavender, and then to white or crushed strawberry, and then to the mystical colour of black to purple.

The variegated green to white lily is lovely but possibly much more common is the 'Green Goddess' arum lily, sometimes seen, regardless of the colour, the shape of both arum and Zantedeschia are magnificent flowers and ideal for the cut flower industry.

As many readers will realise, the lily shape is a bract or modified leaf, and we as flower arrangers, use these leaves in place of flowers in many designs.

Not only is the colour of these remarkable plants interesting to work with, but also when making full use of the leaves of the plant in all design work, this can add interest and visual momentum to any floral art piece of work.

Incredible Orchids...

Cymbidium orchids are incredible indoor plants. A good healthy plant gives a good number of flower spikes that are an ideal asset used in the flower industry. They can be used for bridal work, gift baskets and flower arranging in both modern and traditional design, but they also make good value when buying flowers for the home.

With such a generous display shown by the Orchid Society of Great Britain, there was a great deal to learn and appreciate.

The orchid, (Orchidaceous) plants are distinctive in consisting mostly of perennial, terrestrial or epiphytic herbs.[1]

The orchid that comes directly to mind, is the vanilla bean orchid, or 'V planifolia, grown for its commercial use. Having said that, there were many different orchids on the stand at this year's show.

---

[1] Epiphytic: orchids grow on another plant, especially one that is not parasitic which include: ferns, bromeliads, and air plants

Not only did the stand offer a good selection of plants on display, but so many different varieties not normally seen at the local garden centre or in local florist shops. That is understandable as many plants are rare, one in particular is the Caladenia discoidea, which is said to be 'the ultimate expression of floral deceit...'

These plants have developed their colouring and shape that lures insects to feast on the nectar they produce. 'Visual, tactile, or olfactory signals from the plant suggest the presence of a female insect. In some instances, the plant may ejaculate, thus adding to the confusion by the insects who visit it. That orchid is found in Australian terrestrial areas.

There are currently over 100,000 hybrids, and cultivars with 28,000 species of orchids found worldwide, and yet, there may be many more to be discovered...!

Oh, and Then There Were Tulips…!

Tulips were originally found in Asia, where they were first cultivated by the people of Turkey as early as twelve hundred years ago.

The origin of the name is also Turkish and originated from the word 'turban'.

Like so many different species of plants, tulips were introduced to Europe in the 16th Century.

They then became popular in the Netherlands, where they are associated to today.

It is not only the colour and shape that attracts people to these popular flowers, but they are also edible, this is unlike the daffodil, which is not edible…!

Tulips are a member of the onion and garlic family, having said that, if eaten, the bulbs may cause gastrointestinal distress, nausea, and vomiting.

Like the bulbs, it is not advisable to eat either the stem or the leaves of the plant.

Tulip petals may be used for garnishing on cupcakes, and, or, on many celebration cakes.

With such displays, not only of single-petal flowers, but those now being introduced in the double or multi-petal varieties.

The above photograph gives a stunning collection of multi-petalled blooms and showcases the advancement in shape, form, and colour these beautiful flowers have become, in the 21st Century. 'Sugar Crystal' the name given to the delightful specimens below, would make perfect wedding or celebration flowers.

Gladiolus

Happy smiles and a delight to speak with the women in the above photograph, who were both from Pheasant Acre Plants. They were informative about their gladiolus plants and the gladiolus on display.

Unfortunately, we could not buy any bulbs as we needed to travel back to Australia, and Australia, like so many countries have strict Border controls for any form of flora, fauna and organic materials coming into the country, and that is understandable!

Just the same, I would have loved to 'buy up big… on the bulbs on offer!

With such splendid and vibrant colours, these blooms were a crowd pleaser to everyone that saw them.

Can you imagine so many colours within one variety of flowers…? And opposite, this beautiful salmon pink, always popular in the flower trade.

I can remember, when I first came to Australia, I made many gladioli roses from this colour.

I still think, if brides want to choose a single wedding flower to carry on their wedding day, there is nothing nicer than a single white gladiolus rose with trailing ivy for simplicity and beauty, they may also be affordable…!

Having said that, there are many floristry techniques that have been lost in the effort to cut costs and to create wedding bouquets quickly and affordably.

Sunshine and Lilies – Who Could Ask for More…?

How majestic these flowers have become; they are used as single flower stems in a bud vase or in great profusion in large hotel foyers. They do not only create a grand entrance but give the feeling of opulence, luxury, and wellbeing.

Not only do they give us visual excitement, but the perfume can send our senses into confusion, almost intoxicating us to the point of feeling 'heady, and happy'…

Harts Nursery had a breath-taking collection of colours and both single and double flowering lilies at this year's show.

My goodness, opposite, who could doubt the beauty of these pretty, pink-edged double flowering lilies? With such a display, they almost suggest they are a little piece of heaven sent to keep us happy and safe in time a of uncertainty as our world and its people go through many imposed and different changes.

From pastel colours to fire and fervour, when seeing such a display, the colours excite and calm the human spirit!

From mass displays to single blooms, all are beautiful specimens of achievement...!

It is a privilege to take these beautiful photographs and to have the honour of being able to speak and write about these magnificent blooms.

Dahlia Beach...

With over 4,000 dahlias for the season planted, Dahlia Beach is in full flow creating a kaleidoscope of colour at Chelsea this year.

From picking your own dahlias, to parties, and flower arranging, all is on offer at the venue of Dahlia Beach.

You can take a picnic, explore the farm, shop, enjoy the lake, or have a coffee at the café, there are no limits to having a fun and enjoyable day.[2]

---

[2] Photographs, courtesy of https://www.dahliabeach.co.uk/pyo-dahlias

Iris Or Flag Iris...?

As a child growing up in England, I can remember iris flowers growing in gardens and on rubbish tips, but those days are long since gone.

The planting of iris in gardens goes back to about 1469 BC at the time of King Thutmose III of ancient Egypt.[3]

The King was an enthusiastic gardener and would covet plants, unlike many kings who would covet gold!

In the conquest of Syria, the King discovered irises growing in great numbers and introduced them into his own garden. The flower soon found influence in Egypt and was much admired by the Egyptian population. Quickly the flower symbolised the renewal of life; the three petals were thought to signify faith, wisdom and valour or great courage.

Over many generations, the iris has provided medicinal remedies and contributed to the perfume industry. It, too, is an ingredient in the making of incense used in religious ceremonies.

---

[3] Iris: A Brief History // Missouri Environment and Garden News Article // Integrated Pest Management, University of Missouri

Since King Thutmose III of Egypt BC, the symbol of the iris has been used both in culture and by many monarchs. The fleur-de-lis, now seen as the national emblem of France, the association of the flower and France is thought to come from the three petals of the iris flower. And as we know now, these petals were thought to symbolise faith, wisdom, and valour.

And today, we see this same emblem used in many crowns worn by the monarchy. The symbol also carries through when seen on robes of state and other ceremonial garments.

The iris has been described as a stylised lily, this may be so, but there are so many differences between the iris and the lily in both shape and flower structure!

The history of the iris and our human attachment to this symbolic flower goes back through many generations. Not only do we see the

fleur-de-lis related to the British Monarchy but to the French or Franks as they were then known.

The Franks before conquering Gaul in 486 AD lived for a time, around the river of Lys, in Flanders. The river was bordered with yellow iris flowers, where these flowers still grow today.

Though the flowers around the river are yellow, this is not seen as an iris colour, it is the symbolic shape of the three petals sweeping downwards and the three reaching upwards that has inspired the eternal shape of the much-used fleur-de-lis as national symbols used by both the British and French to date. The symbol is seen on ceremonial occasions, within embroidery into robes or as part of the fine gold and artwork, worked into and through a crown's design.

And so, it is today, the fleur-de-lis is seen on wallpapers, laminated onto clothing, including tee shirts and women's dresses, woven into fabrics including dress fabrics, and woven into carpet and rug designs. The symbol represents tradition, status, and long standing.

Because of the curves in the petal of the iris flower, it makes it a pleasant shape to see and study, therefore, the visual impression becomes a meditative experience.

The Iris

The iris, with petals like the sails of a ship…
standing tall and not wanting to tip….

For when the wind blows, the time will come
when the sails are fragile and old…

Not standing to be seen, magnificent and bold…
The petals of which are significant you see…

For the petals always grow within three…
From knights and king's past, the iris has meant:
Faith, wisdom and valour and a great sign of strength…!

From distant times and up to today
The iris is resplendent in all that I say…

And it is again, my imagination it captures, and words cannot explain…
how my heart lingers through cold winter months
for the sight of this flower and what relief it brings when one is in pain…!

Yes, from the times of the Romans and Greeks, and before
so many, the ancient Egyptians we're told…

This flower has held wonder to their sights as the petals unfold…!

From yellows to whites, purples, and pinks, and to dazzle us,
with beauty, and unable to think…!

For the sails of the ship, that once did we see,
as the season lingers and autumn is near

We know the iris shall soon disappear…

As time does not stand still, it's with heavy heart,
I write these words…

Lingering in thought for the next time I see,
the flower that is perfect and captures my gaze…

Though from a distance, the thoughts are within,
if I look for a while, the iris appears, and a new life begins …!

The Pleasure of Delphiniums

Delphiniums were in splendour at this year's show and today, we see the outcome of many years of work by delphinium growers. With over 300 species across the world, their beauty and their use in the cut flower industry continues to be developed.

The word delphinium originated from the Greek word delphin, meaning dolphin. The flower's spur resembles the dolphin's back when seen swimming through the water. In Greek mythology, the flowers bloomed from the blood of Ajax, the son of Telamon and cousin of Achilles. He was brave, strong, and played a pivotal role in the Trojan War.

With nearly 40 different colours and over 300 species worldwide, there are many to choose from. It isn't any wonder that we love to see them in our homes, in tall, elegant arrangements for display and event purposes and for show in many flower shops.

'Constance Rivett' is a pure white delphinium with a white eye and makes a superb wedding flower in both wedding bouquets or used in flower displays for decoration at a church or wedding venue.

Delphiniums are part of the Ranunculaceae family which includes buttercups, columbines, and monkshood.

Wild delphinium is found in the Northern hemisphere, and the mountainous ranges of tropical Africa. Delphinium is also known as larkspur. Having worked and owned businesses in the flower industry, to a florist, the words delphinium and larkspur relate to two different tall flower types, both of which are used in commercial floristry.

Despite its beauty and appeal, delphinium is a poisonous plant. After working with the flowers, wash your hands. Delphinium is no different to many plants we decorate our homes or workplaces with; if we want to use their beauty to enhance our lives, we need to understand that their beauty comes about by the genetics they inherit; the genetic makeup of plants is designed to ensure their survival.

In the above, at this year's show, the colours of the delphiniums are enhanced by the accompanying and sharp contrasted begonia flowers.

Amazing Maple...

Acer, commonly known as Maple are believed to have originated in China. They are now dispersed through Asia, Europe, Northern Africa, and parts of the Southern Hemisphere, including Australia.

Recognition of the maple usually relates to the shape of their palmate shaped leaves. Their closest relative being the Horse Chestnut.

Maples have a sweet sugary sap which was used to sweeten foods by the Northern American Indians.

These beautiful trees show their exciting colours during autumn, and the display at this year's show was breathtaking and the colour spectacular.

The Water Garden

Nestled within the Great Pavilion, we were surprised to see this amazing aquatic garden full of different aquatic plants, including some green aquatic grasses, flowering plants, and many different shaped leaf plants all of which add great interest to any pond setting.

The audience too, were enjoying the display. The water was kept in place by 200 x 100mm oak, possibly treated pine or a sustainable material used in the retaining walls which proved to be effective in appearance and structure.

With such a use of materials, it gives us the idea, we can create our water feature gardens in almost any location.

The water was not only calming to see, but the effective use of beautiful plants added to the ambiance of the display.

The Salad Bowl

With such a selection of edible salad greens and assorted herbs on display; it was a remarkable collection of almost designer foods, some of which were organic, and that is always good to know.

Brighter Blooms of Lancashire left 'no stone unturned' when displaying their products for healthy eating and living. It's great to see the turnaround in produce taking place; we are now becoming aware of how good eating relates back to good health and wellbeing.

Old Fashioned Violas are Back and in Abundance...!

What is it about these little treasures that makes your heart happy? Their faces are exquisite, and they show a smile to you every time you look at them.

From lavender to white, a bit of yellow-to lemon here and there and then there is this remarkable display of treasures, with many, held memories from many people's childhoods I should imagine!

Is it any wonder, this display won the 'Silver Gilt Medal' at the Show?

Most violas are found in temperate climates of the Northern Hemisphere, some in Hawaii and in areas within Australia and the Andes.

Some have a sweet perfume, and the scent is part of their enticing appeal.

Violas and violets have been cultivated since ancient times and used for medicinal purposes, perfumes, and colouring. Violets dipped in a sugar solution can be used in decorating cakes, or unsugared may be added to salads and used as ornamental decoration on food dishes.

Shots of Magic

From gasps of pleasure to the excitement of seeing a magnitude of colour in one spot allows the eyes and brain to feast on the sight seen.

Masses of flowers, coloured foliage, the dominant one being Coleus which can be easily grown from a cutting.

Pretty Gardens...

Keeping oneself on track while visiting each garden, taking notes, and photographs, and using all our human senses, we collect the information we need to create this beautiful book.

It is not only our recall we rely on, but the excitement of the day, the visit to the show and our love of the event each year.

Soft colours, soothing greens and the fine foliage shapes all help bring together this amazing collection developed to stimulate the human senses and this it does.

So many of the plants are familiar to my childhood, and I am sure to many of our readers memories.

There was a profusion of colour, shape, and form as we were ready to see the next visual delight.

With soft dancing yellows, touches of orange, lavender and pink colours, and the tiny faces of daisies, all help to bring home to us the importance of protecting our wildflowers, thus allowing our native animals and insects the food they need.

Great news, old fashioned lupins flowers were seen at several stands at the show. Not only are they colourful and make wonderful displays in the garden, but the lupin seed is gaining favour as an alternative food source to soy!

With a greater number of people on the planet to feed, the lupin seed offers many benefits. The seed known as the lupin bean, can be used in different foods, as a flake, or flour. The bean contains a full range of amino acids, contrary to the soybean.

Lupin flour can be made into bread and cake foods. It is high in protein, is naturally gluten-free and low in fat.

Lupins can be grown in temperate climates and are increasingly becoming known as a cash crop for farmers. Our lupins offer many other benefits, once established and in bloom, they offer a bountiful food larder for our pollinating insects, including the bees.

Masses of ground covering orchids including cypripediums of different types and the lily Arisaema Sikokianum, also known as the Japanese Cobra Lily is seen in the below photograph.

Because of the white-on-white colours in the flower, you will notice the dark outer flower reveals the inside white large, swollen sex organ (spadix) of the flower. The spadix provides a deep contrast to the flower when compared to the dark purple petal, (spathe).

The plant grows well in well-drained, dry soil. The plant remains striking until it goes dormant in late summer when it then rests until the next season.

It's an ideal plant for a woodland garden.

Opposite photograph courtesy Wiki Commons.

While I was the appointed florist at the Prime Ministers Lodge, Canberra, Australia, one of the plants growing in the gardens of the Lodge, were the below Solomons Seal. I love this for floral design work.

The natural bend in the plant offers a great opportunity to use the flower stem from the back so that full beauty of the bell-shaped flowers can be seen.

The tiny flowers are hardy and if wired separately, can be used in headdress design and in small wedding bouquets; they are a lot of work, but are a different approach to other flowers more readily used in wedding work.

The last time I worked with these delightful flowers was at the Prime Minister's Lodge, and in flower arrangements for Queen Elizabeth ll's visit on her Australian tour in 1980.

Different Gardens – Different Approaches to Gardening

It appears that clipped lawns and sharp garden edges are becoming ideas of the past, and now we are seeing consideration for animal and insect habitats.

Giving back our gardens to the little creatures that help to keep our gardens and soil healthy is just one small step forward.

It's refreshing to see the emphasis on small but healthy environments, not only for the natural wildlife and environment but also for us humans…!

Understanding that the good environments we each create pays us back in many ways. When our children can grow and play in healthy gardens, we too, feel that benefit.

If we grow our own vegetables in healthy soils, we again feel the benefit.

By taking small steps to create a healthy garden and environment, we will all gain the benefits.

Different Combinations & Peace of Mind...

With layers of different field and wildflowers in our gardens, we too, can enjoy the natural beauty that each season brings.

With changing colours in the seasons to the different textures that help to give us a visual smorgasbord of delight.

Ranunculi to buttercups, and alliums and then to purple iris, all have intrigue and fascination for our senses and good mental health.

Taking the time to look, see, experience and wonder pays dividends in giving us the ability to find peace, tranquillity, and solace within our busy lives.

Sweet Peas

As pretty as they are, the pea of the sweet pea is not good for human consumption. The only living beings to enjoy these pods and their peas are aphids, snails, caterpillars, and some rabbits.

Having said the above, we should enjoy the cultivated and wild sweet peas as they are a truly fragile and beautiful flower.

Who Remembers Wallflowers?

The heady fragrance of summer as I played in my grandmother's garden in Sussex in England came rushing back to me as I saw this stand at the show.

It was lovely to see these old-fashioned flowers again, and it seems, there are double blooms now…!

Fresh and clean, the colours and foliage and looking deeply into the bottom photograph, the traditional reddish-brown colour is seen.

In the bottom photograph, you can see is a nice sharp citrus yellow. There may have been more of these delightful flowers, but we were limited for time and the day was long….!

Let's hope, by this first appearance, it's a sign of more to come. It was an absolute treat to see these gems make an appearance.

Gardens to Capture Dreams

How nice is it, to stop and dream? The beautiful displays in the below photographs give us that opportunity, to stop, take a moment and just enjoy.

Each flower, each leaf that grows are all visual gifts for us to enjoy, if we do not see their beauty, that is our missed opportunity that will not come again!

Splendid Grasses

The stand wins Gold, and with so much emphasis on the need to manage and look after our environment, it is not a surprise that grasses have taken a big leap forward with the national awareness of and to global warming.

It is the preservation of what we have and how to enjoy and work with the natural world that is going to keep humankind safe.

This picture-perfect photograph of the grasses on display is one of the reasons it makes a long-haul flight so worthwhile.

Bonsai and Perfection

How many years of dedication does it take to create such magnificent miniature growing trees?

The art of growing small trees goes back to ancient China, and the year, 700 CE. The Chinese were using superior techniques to create dwarf trees in containers.

Originally this artform was only practised by the elite society of China. As the years passed, the Japanese also adopted the ancient art and indeed, the art of Bonsai creation is associated with Japan today. Bonsai are certainly living works of art and greatly admired throughout the world.

Bonsai is the Japanese word, meaning, 'tree in a pot'. The miniature trees are grown and have the representation of nature.

Depending on the culture associated to the creator of the tree, the tree represents and symbolises, harmony, patience, in some instances, luck, and balance.

In some religions, the bonsai represents meditation and contemplation.

The fascination of early explorers in ancient China when discovering miniature trees with their stunted and gnarled trunks in high alpine areas may have been the start of this art form. Taoist Monks, as early as the 4th Century BCE believed in recreating nature. Many people may have also believed the shapes may contain magical properties.

The art of bonsai is also recreated in many painted artworks on porcelain, in pictures, on fabrics and other impressions where the bonsai image is used.

There is also a connection to, and within human thinking, to the bonsai shaping of tree branches, many animal impressions and in yoga positions. Accordingly, the first pictorial indication of creative tree miniaturisation was found in 706 CE in the tomb of Prince Zhang Huai.

Within this article, we can only feature some of the amazing bonsai on display. As can be seen, small flowering trees can also be trained into stunning shapes and, at the right time of year, come into flower.

There are many trees that can be made into bonsai, here are some: Crepe Myrtle, Hibiscus, Apple, Maple, Azalea, Bougainvillea, Cape Honeysuckle, Cherry, Pomegranate and Wisteria.

With an interest in creating wellbeing in our lifestyles, the hobby of creating bonsai would support the knowledge, identifying the stillness of the mind, the quiet meditation of self, and the deep and satisfying experience of watching a living tree grow into its natural and beautiful shape.

Of course, if a seasonal tree was chosen, such as maple, there would also be the natural and seasonal changes that would take place giving added colour and enjoyment to the experience…!

Another Reign Begins...

In last year's book, we saw this amazing impression of her late Majesty, Queen Elizabeth ll, by Ming Veevers Carter. It was an incredible capture, created through clever flower placements, of the image of the late Queen.

The photograph was shot in the late afternoon, hence the light in the background.

This year, the Scottish Plants Company, Binny, has created the intricate crown image below for the new Monarch, King Charles lll.

The intricate bringing together of stripped vine and branches are woven into different parts of the crown creating different textures within the shape.

When comparing the size of the creation with the gentleman in the photograph, it brings home the size and volume of the design.

It is indeed a study and there needs to be time to appreciate the work undertaken to create such a masterpiece.

Garden Accessories

The Ornate Garden Company displayed some of its designs at the show. From designs that go from completely round spheres to offset and oval shapes.

These small, but separate rooms could have many uses in the garden, from an extra reading room and small library, to adding a small and separate dining room, the only limitation in its use is thinking, 'how can I make use of this delightful added addition to our garden?'

The opposite interior shows the pretty and positive contribution such an outside addition can make to any garden or outside setting. One of the suggestions made was to add an outside business, office, or study area, while another was to make such a room into a small nursery if a person is wanting to start a business.

Depending on personal requirements, this simple idea could be adapted to meet many family or individual needs. Please keep in mind Council Planning.

The Ancient Art of Pebble Laying

The ancient art of pebble laying goes back thousands of years. This art was mainly kept for use on pavements and seen firstly in the Eastern Mediterranean areas. From the Mediterranean to Asia Minor where this artform has been seen on excavated floors from the 7th and 8th centuries BC.

By looking at the top photograph, one is drawn to the intricate use of shadowing by grading the pebbles in different tonal values.

It was incredible to see this art in revival and with such detailed images, one, the image of a flying bee in the distant, opposite photograph. With such details, in the produced work, and all created by grading the pebbles by colour and shape.

These are not only remarkable pieces of skilled artwork, but so appropriate in this time of global awareness to the plight of our insects but in the use of collected pebbles, from their natural environment that gives pleasure to all who have the good fortune to see the images.

Interesting Stalls
The Delphinium Society

We have written on the delphinium plant and its flowers earlier in the book. Having said that, the Delphinium Society, by its creation of the pretty stall is worth a mention here.

By the attractive and novel approach of a shop front, the Delphinium Society have created the feeling of, 'I want to enter here to see what this is all about...!'

The use of the colours of lovely English garden in mid-summer was beautiful to see.

Susan Entwistle Art

Susan Entwistle

The superb use of vibrant colours in, not only the artwork of the paintings, but by utilising the art in the making of other products such as cushions, gift cards, baubles, and other forms of gifts, makes Susan's artwork multi-purposed.

The original paintings are beautiful. Susan captures the scenes in the, pointlist style of modernism, which makes her work extraordinary. Susan seizes the colourful combinations of the seasons, which, in turn, captures the imagination and is completely playful on the mind.

When looking at the paintings, it's difficult not to smile, to feel happy and the sunshine of the moment.

Bee The Change

Caring for our bees and insects must be a priority as we move more into the global awareness, that the planet is under threat.

A Scottish Charity Foundation, 'Bee The Change', and within the heading, the Bumblebee Conservation Trust, is helping to raise awareness about the plight of the bumblebee and the need to protect its habitat.

In the spring, the bumblebee queens appear from hibernation and start to look for a safe home that is dry, sheltered, and safe where she can raise her young. As humans create more building sites, fewer nesting sites become less available. These bees do an amazing job in fertilising wildflowers, and crops, therefore, they need our help. For more information and the website, please see below.[4]

---

[4] Homepage - Bee The Change | Bumblebee Conservation Trust

Mr Fothergill's...

Mr Fothergill's offers flower and vegetable seed ranges in partnership with the RHS. Mr Fothergill's has grown from humble beginnings to become one of the biggest European suppliers of seed to the hobby garden market ...

An extraordinary stall, with old-world charm....

Containers Made from Husks

The sooner, we the consumers, are not using plastics, we all know, our planet will be in a much better place!

With remnants of the Industrial Revolution and the great move forward into using synthetics in clothing, furniture, children's toys, household goods, food, and drink containers to mention only a few, it is a relief to see the food husk being re-cycled into usable objects.

The company 'Husk' creates usable house and kitchen utensils and containers, cookware and tableware from the biodegradable agricultural bi-product waste that are eco-friendly and plastic free.

With the few items seen in the above photograph, we can see just how versatile the husk can be if used in everyday home items. That may just be the starting point, as a mum and grandmother, it would be great for me to see children's toys made of something other than plastic…!

The Peony Girl

'Fun and carefree...' is how the Peony Girl describes her artwork. With so many beautiful paintings to see, which are truly wonderful, it would be difficult to not see the smiles the work brings to its viewers.

Siyuan, pronounced 'see you anne', loves peony flowers and has spent her life in China, Europe, including the Netherlands and Britain.

She enjoys the challenges her work brings to her. From trying new techniques, some of which work, some do not, each offer Siyuan a new opportunity to learn about her art. She doesn't let the challenge deter her and often works with a difficult task to make it work for her. In the process, she creates different and beautiful paintings of the peony flower.

The peony flower is not only a beautiful flower but is regarded as the national flower of China.

Clothes of the Future

Clothes made from roots of plants in the future cannot be ruled out.

From the photographer and artist, Zena Holloway, we have a great alternative to fabrics made from synthetic materials. Zena grows grass roots, which are environmentally friendly, to make her fabric.

These fabrics are a great leap forward and have many advantages for the textile industries and the world of fashion.

When looking at the above dress design, it is easy to see how this material can so easily fit into the fashion industry.

Taking the idea even further, such fabrics could be made for the higher end of the fashion industry, including wedding and evening gowns. Once developed, such a material could be used in everyday clothing.

When we stop to think about the ancient Egyptians and their use of flax to create their linen clothing, it gives us multiple ideas. Linen is a fabric that allows the body to naturally breathe, is cool to wear, and has hard wearing benefits. Fabrics made from natural root would also offer this human benefit of body comfort.

For different ideas to fashion, we have included the above photograph, which may allow the synthetic textile industry to re-invent itself![5]

---

[5] Photograph, courtesy ZenHolloway.com

With such amazing ideas and creations coming from Zena Holloway, the artist, maker, and material innovator, it is remarkable to see how roots, which grow all over the world, can be used in textile production.

It is not only the use of the root in clothing, but the world population benefits with such ideas, and this can be a great advantage to us all.

Remarkable clothing designs, which can be used in so many ways, are inventive and forward thinking put into action to create the outcome which you see in these photographs.

Treats of the Show

With each show exhibit there were visual surprises in store. In the photographs in this section, we are introducing some delightful flower exhibits that can truly stand alone.

Not greatly used in the flower industry, this beautiful plant and its flowers offer versatility, lasting strength, and a variety of colours from white, to different blues and now there is 'Agapanthus Blackjack', as seen in the photograph opposite.

With all tones of purples being highly popular with brides, will this flower and its colour become a 'must have' for future wedding flowers?

Blackjack has large heads with purple striped blooms.

The plant is recommended for borders and use in containers, the flower industry should not be forgotten as the colour will add a great dimension to the florist when they suggest the use of this flower and its colour…!

Above, this delightful sunflower with its inner golden glow at the base of the petals is just one exhibit. It was in itself, a showstopper.

Above the delightful pink of the Hydrangea serrata, (Euphoria Pink), was the second and runner up, in Plant of the Year exhibits. With a foliage that flushes pink, white, and green and two-toned flowers of white to a hot ruby and pale centres, it was exquisite.

Then, there were the rose exhibits, such delicate colours and displays, they did indeed allow the mind to take a rest, mellow until the next delightful exhibit was seen.

And then below, we see the European Peony flower, and what a spectacle it was to see...?

Soft petals to equal the wings of a butterfly with warm and inviting centre pieces of invitations to insects to come and feast and fertilize while the flower shows off its fragile beauty to all who take the time to stop and look...!

An absolute delight and privilege to see such beautiful flower specimens.

Opposite, 'Californian Poppies' are an old-fashioned garden plant often seen in many gardens in Britain and Europe during the summer months.

Despite its long acquaintance to, the flower gardens, upon its arrival in and when it shows its flowers, it's always a time of sunshine, long, warm evenings and a time of enjoyment in the British and European gardens.

The Californian Poppy was originally native to Northern California and Southern Mexico but is now grown in many other parts of the world. It is a member of the Ranunculus family and is greatly prized by the Native Americans for its medicinal value.

Opposite, the plant 'Dame's Rocket', or Mother of the Evening, or Sweet Rocket or Wild Phlox is a sweet, scented plant that releases a wonderful perfume on summer evenings.

When walking past this plant and if brushed by clothing, the perfume seems to intensify; it can leave lasting and good memories of summer…!

Opposite, this large-leaved lupin grows to about 50-100cm. In flower it attracts many pollinating insects, including bees.

The lupin is used in many informal, cottage gardens where the true grandeur of the flower columns can be seen and show off.

Covering a range of different colours from the deep reds to apricots, pinks, and a range of blues, they are an ideal summer flower, however, they are considered invasive in some countries and regions of the world.

Below, the ivy geranium is always a great asset in any garden whether grown in the garden or flowerpot; they are hardy and seem to withstand tough forgetting to water!

When loved, they show their appreciation by giving us a spectacular display of lasting and colourful flowers; they are very forgiving plants…!

The Reason Why...?
The Magic of Chelsea

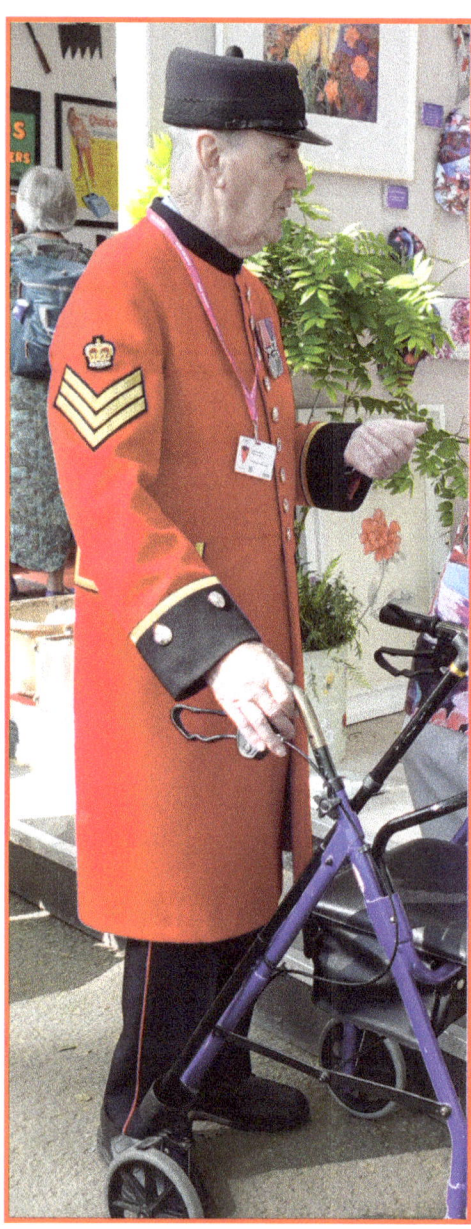

Thank you for the wonderful conversations, friendship, and fun we experienced on our one short day during our visit to the United Kingdom.

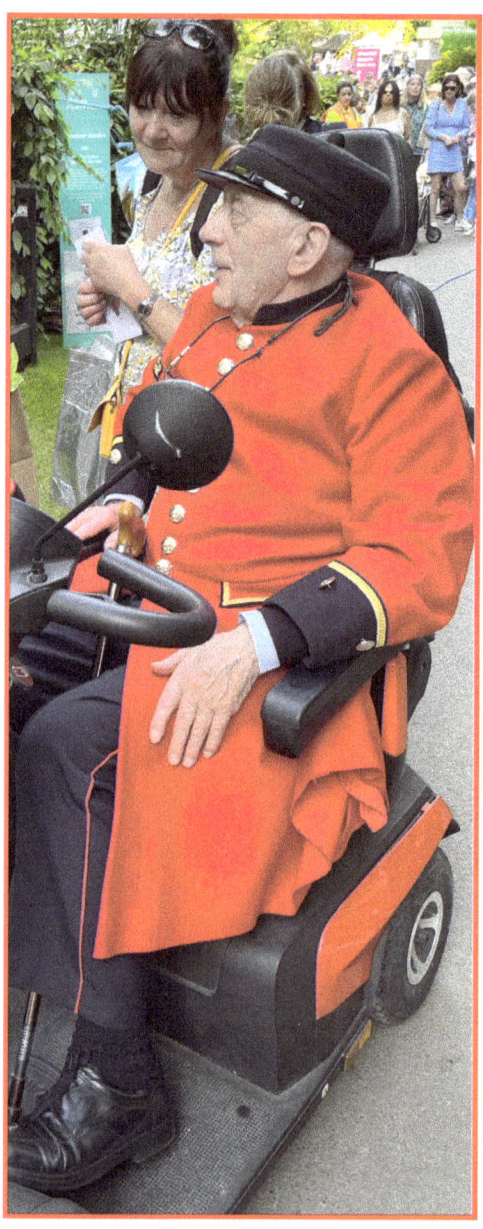

Emblem, Courtesy, The Royal Hospital Chelsea, Home of the Chelsea Pensioners.

Other Books That May Interest You

Available Online
www.how2books.com.au

The book, 'How To Create Easy Wedding Bouquets', introduces you to many techniques in wedding bouquet construction, the different methods used to wire different flowers and leaves, how to tape, ribboning the wedding bouquet handle, how to make a corsage, buttonhole and other industry techniques that will start you on a floristry career.

Our education company, Full Potential Education And Training has been developed to support people who want to learn how to build skills for the floristry industry. The course is a CPD Accredited 20-week online course in commercial floristry wedding bouquet making. It has been designed to support people who want to work for themselves and start a business or for those people who want a trade career in the floristry industry. For more information, please email, admin@fullpotentialtraining.com.au

The book, 'How To Create Easy Flower Arrangements', is an introduction to floral art and commercial floristry in flower arranging. The book is designed to help those people who want to learn flower arranging and construction techniques and will give the foundation knowledge to those people who want to work in the floristry industry.

It will also help people who want to learn flower arranging for pleasure and gift giving, and those people who create flower arrangements for special occasions.

The Magic of Chelsea, 2022, is full of information covering the Chelsea Flower Show, floristry, art and design, sculpture, different plants and how they are used and has other informative and relevant information that gives the reader different information about the topics included. It would be an ideal book for florists, garden centres, nurseries and like businesses to have as a book for sale in their business. For wholesale information, please email: admin@booksforreadingonline.com

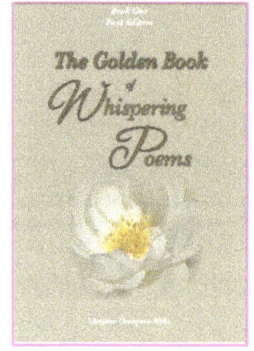
Because we love the books we create, and poetry is a big part of the work we do, we could not help ourselves but include this book of different poetry.

Without plants, we cannot survive. As all flower and lovers know, many plants and trees are under threat! Plants not only help to keep our planet and wildlife healthy, but they also add to our human wellbeing.

This book outlines the benefits of using herbs in our everyday lives. It is colourful and gives a breakdown of herb uses.

All the books are available at
www.how2books.com.au
This book is brought to you from the publishers of:

ISBN: 978-0-6457284-7-7

www.ingramcontent.com/pod-product-compliance
Lightning Source LLC
Chambersburg PA
CBHW061536010526
44107CB00066B/2880